STEGOSAURUS

A TRUE BOOK

by
Elaine Landau

Children's Press®
A Division of Grolier Publishing
New York London Hong Kong Sydney
Danbury, Connecticut

An artist's
impression of
Stegosaurus

Reading Consultant
Linda Cornwell
*Coordinator Of School Quality
And Professional Improvement
Indiana State Teachers Association*

Science Consultant
Dr. Kenneth Carpenter
*Denver Museum of
Natural History*

Author's Dedication:
To Barbara Soto

Visit Children's Press® on the Internet at:
http://publishing.grolier.com

Library of Congress Cataloging-in-Publication Data

Landau, Elaine.
    Stegosaurus / by Elaine Landau.
       p.   cm. — (A True Book)
    Summary: Describes the characteristics and habits of the plant-
eating dinosaur, as well as theories about why dinosaurs became extinct.
    ISBN 0-516-20452-1 (lib.bdg.)   0-516-26505-9 (pbk.)
    1. Stegosaurus—Juvenile literature. [1. Stegosaurus.
    2. Dinosaurs.] I. Title. II. Series.
    QE862.065L37 1999
    567.915'3—dc21
                                                         98-8278
                                                         CIP
                                                         AC

Contents

Stegosaurus facing off against Tyrannosaurus rex

Traveling Back in Time

What if you had a time machine and could travel back in time? Where would you go? Would you want to see the Age of the Dinosaurs? If so, you would set your travel dial to the Mesozoic era. This time period lasted from 245 million years ago to 65 million years ago. Stop your machine after going back about 150 million years in time. Park your time machine and look around. You are in the Jurassic period, the middle period of the Mesozoic era. This is a time when many different dinosaurs roamed the Earth, including an unusual-looking one called *Stegosaurus*.

What were dinosaurs? Dinosaurs were ancient reptiles that lived on land. Like all

Stegosaurus lived in North America more than 150 million years ago.

reptiles, dinosaurs had scaly or leathery skin, lungs, and young that hatched from eggs with shells.

7

It won't be hard to spot *Stegosaurus.* It's a large dinosaur with shieldlike plates on parts of its body. These plates point straight up into the air.

Stegosaurus was a member of a large family of dinosaurs known as stegosaurids. Like *Stegosaurus*, all of them had some type of bony plating. To see other stegosaurids, you would have to visit Africa, India, Europe, or China.

This museum exhibit shows how the land may have looked when *Stegosaurus* roamed the Earth.

Stegosaurus was the largest of the stegosaurids, and the only one that lived in North America.

Fossils

Paleontologists are scientists who study prehistoric life. They learn about dinosaurs from fossils. These are animal or plant remains, such as bones or teeth, that have been buried in the Earth's crust for millions of years. Some fossils within rocks have

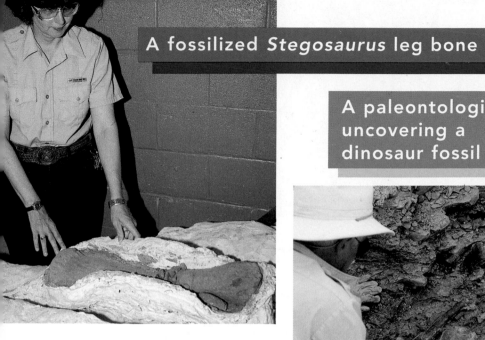

A fossilized *Stegosaurus* leg bone

A paleontologist uncovering a dinosaur fossil

been exposed from the wearing-away action of rain, wind, and rivers. In rarer cases, fossils have been discovered inside rocks that have been quarried—cut or blasted apart.

Some of the earliest *Stegosaurus* fossils were found at this site in Morrison, Colorado.

Paleontologists have been able to figure out what different dinosaurs looked like by putting fossilized bones back together again. It's sort of like putting together pieces from a puzzle!

Paleontologist O. C. Marsh named *Stegosaurus* in 1877, after discovering fossils in

A *Stegosaurus* skeleton displayed in the position in which it was found

Morrison, Colorado. A nearly complete *Stegosaurus* skeleton was uncovered in 1886 in Fremont County, Colorado. Today it is housed in the Smithsonian Institution in Washington, D.C. The skeleton is displayed in the position in which it was found.

Who Was *Stegosaurus?*

If you could really travel back in time to North America, where would you find *Stegosaurus*? You'd probably see this slow-moving dinosaur roaming through Colorado, Utah, and Wyoming. Millions of years ago, that was *Stegosaurus* territory.

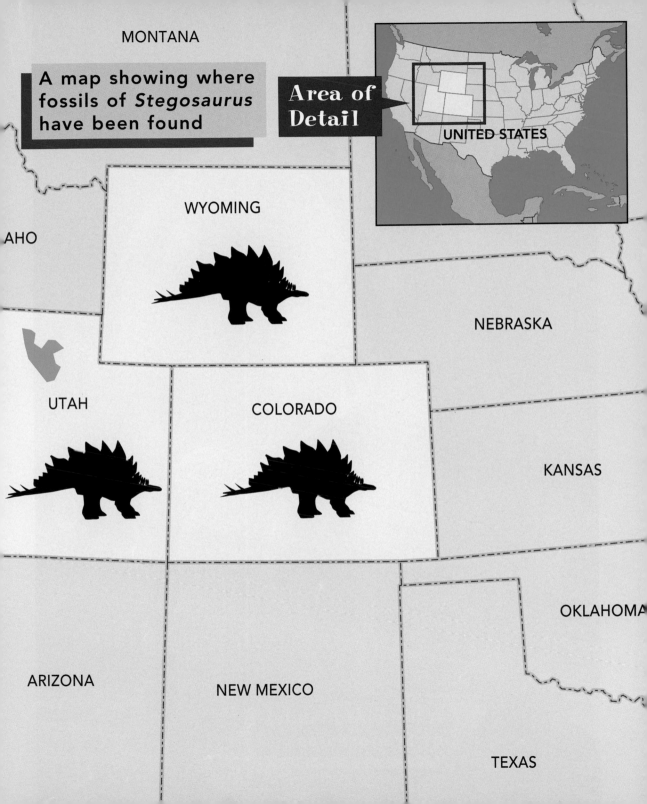

A map showing where fossils of *Stegosaurus* have been found

Area of Detail

UNITED STATES

MONTANA

WYOMING

AHO

UTAH

COLORADO

NEBRASKA

KANSAS

ARIZONA

NEW MEXICO

OKLAHOMA

TEXAS

A life-sized model of *Stegosaurus*

Have you ever visited these states? Perhaps you live there now or did when you were younger. In prehistoric times, *Stegosaurus* might have wandered down a bicycle path you now use. Or maybe it looked for food in your backyard. Imagine looking out your window and seeing a 5-ton, 25-foot (8-m-) long *Stegosaurus* instead of the family dog.

Yet *Stegosaurus* looked somewhat unusual even for the

Jurassic period. Perhaps its strangest feature was the double row of bony plates jutting out from its neck, back, and tail.

Shaped like arrowheads, the largest plates were about 3 feet (1 m) tall. *Stegosaurus's* throat was covered with numerous small, bony disks as well. Some *Stegosaurus* also had disk-shaped shields or plates over their hips.

Stegosaurus had bony, shieldlike plates along its back.

It is not hard to see why this dinosaur was named *Stegosaurus*, which means "roofed dinosaur." Its plating looked like roof tiles. Some early researchers thought that the bony plates made *Stegosaurus* look more like an armored tank than an animal. Not surprisingly, it is also known as one of the "armored dinosaurs."

A close-up view of a *Stegosaurus* skeleton showing the bony plates

At the end of *Stegosaurus*'s tail were pairs of large, sharply pointed spikes. Each of these was 2 to 3 feet (0.6 to 1 m) long.

Stegosaurus shown with its plates
directly across from one another

Stegosaurus skeleton shown
with staggered plates

Plate Position?

Since no *Stegosaurus* skeleton has ever been found with its bony plates attached, no one is really sure how the plates were arranged. Most paleontologists agree that the plates were arranged in two rows along the back. But some think that the plates were directly across from one another, while others think the plates were staggered. That's why some paintings or reconstructed skeletons of *Stegosaurus* look one way, and some the other!

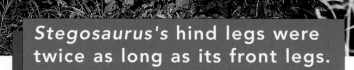

Stegosaurus's hind legs were twice as long as its front legs.

Stegosaurus's large, bulky body was supported by its four strong legs. Its hind legs were twice as long as its front legs. This caused the dinosaur's body to slope forward from its hips to its head.

Stegosaurus's front feet have been compared to an elephant's. Each foot had a sturdy padded base and five short, broad toes. But unlike an elephant, *Stegosaurus* had a blunt claw on each front toe. *Stegosaurus's* hind feet each had three toes with blunt claws.

The bones of a *Stegosaurus* back foot (left) and front foot (below)

The skull of *Stegosaurus*

For such a huge animal, *Stegosaurus* had an unusually small head. Just 16 inches (40 cm) long, it was only a fraction of the size of many of the dinosaur's other body parts. *Stegosaurus's* brain was equally tiny. It was only about the size of a hot dog!

Dinosaur Dining

Stegosaurus was a plant-eating dinosaur. It moved through the forested plains looking for vegetation (plants) to eat. Most paleontologists think that *Stegosaurus* used its low-held head to spot and eat low-growing vegetation.

Stegosaurus probably ate low-growing plants.

Jutting out from the tip of *Stegosaurus*'s snout was a horn-covered beak. The beak was toothless. *Stegosaurus*'s few teeth were located at the back of its mouth.

This close-up view of a *Stegosaurus* model shows how its face may have looked.

These leaf-shaped teeth were quite weak and were not meant for eating meat.

Stegosaurus had teeth only at the very back of its mouth.

Researchers think that *Stegosaurus* may have used its weak jaws and teeth only to pull plant material from the ground or from low-lying shrubs or trees. The dinosaur probably swallowed the plants whole. Such "meals" may have remained in its stomach for several days. There, the food was partially broken down by substances called enzymes.

It's possible that smooth pebbles, called stomach stones, were swallowed by the dinosaur beforehand to aid this process. The pebbles would have torn up the food until it was ready to be digested.

Defense

A dinosaur had to do more than eat to survive. It also needed to fend off predators. As a slow-moving dinosaur, *Stegosaurus* probably could not outrun its enemies. But at times, it may have had to fight off meat eaters larger than itself. It may also have been

Stegosaurus fighting off the meat-eating *Allosaurus*

prey for groups of small meat-eating dinosaurs that attacked in packs.

The spikes at the end of *Stegosaurus*'s tail

Yet *Stegosaurus* was not defenseless. When threatened, it would lash the predator with its spiked, muscular tail. The hard, sharp spikes could rip open its enemy's flesh. Paleontologists also think that *Stegosaurus* may have traveled in herds while on the move. Predators would be less likely to attack large groups of dinosaurs.

Stegosaurus's bony plates may have been used to help fend off attacks. If threatened by a predator or rival male, *Stegosaurus* may have made itself look bigger by turning sideways and displaying its plates, much like an angry cat turning its arched body.

In addition, paleontologists have found a large number of blood-vessel grooves on *Stegosaurus's* plates. This means that a good deal of blood could flow across the surface of the plates beneath the horny covering. This increased blood flow might have caused the plates to "blush," making them stand out sharply against the greens

As this dinosaur-skeleton exhibit shows, *Stegosaurus* may have used its bony plates to scare off such predators as *Allosaurus*.

and tans of the surrounding plant life. The effect would make *Stegosaurus* appear more threatening to both rivals and predators.

Extinction

Some people think that all dinosaurs became extinct at the same time. But it didn't happen quite that way.

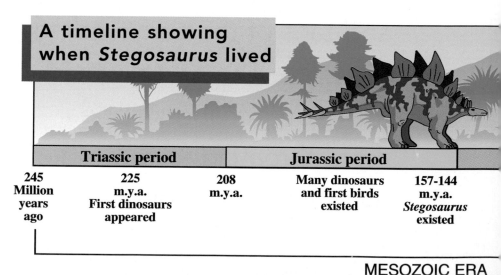

A timeline showing when *Stegosaurus* lived

Triassic period			Jurassic period	
245 Million years ago	225 m.y.a. First dinosaurs appeared	208 m.y.a.	Many dinosaurs and first birds existed	157-144 m.y.a. *Stegosaurus* existed

Various types of dinosaurs
existed at different stages of
the Mesozoic era. No kind of
dinosaur lasted for the whole
time that dinosaurs existed on
Earth. Although the Age of
the Dinosaurs lasted about
150 million years, each type of

(Note: "m.y.a." means "million years ago")

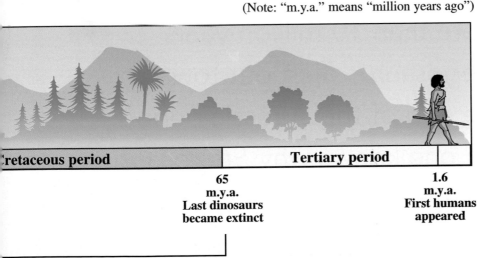

Cretaceous period   Tertiary period

65
m.y.a.
Last dinosaurs
became extinct

1.6
m.y.a.
First humans
appeared

Stegosaurus roamed the Earth for more than 10 million years.

dinosaur existed for only a few million years.

After lasting on Earth for more than 10 million years, *Stegosaurus* died out toward the end of the Jurassic period. No one knows why *Stegosaurus* became extinct when it did.

About 65 million years ago, at the close of the Cretaceous period–long after *Stegosaurus* was gone–all the remaining dinosaurs died out. No one knows for certain what happened. One theory is that a comet or asteroid crashed into Earth. If one of these hit our planet, a huge hole in the ground, called a crater, would be formed. The dust from the crater would float up into the atmosphere. There it would form thick, dark clouds blocking out the Sun. Without the Sun's warmth, Earth's climate would turn quite cold. If this is what happened 65 million years ago, dinosaurs and other forms of life would not have been able to survive this weather change.

We've had a brief look at *Stegosaurus.* Now it's time to climb back into the time machine. Set the dial to return to the future. Maybe our first

A reconstructed *Stegosaurus* skeleton on display in a museum

stop will be a museum or library. There'll be exhibits, films, and other books to help us learn still more about the bony-plated dinosaur called *Stegosaurus*.

To Find Out More

Here are some additional resources to help you learn more about *Stegosaurus:*

Books

Aliki. **Fossils Tell of Long Ago.** Crowell, 1990.

Amazing Dinosaurs: the Fastest, the Smallest, the Fiercest, and the Tallest. Western Publishing Company, 1991.

Cole, Joanna. **The Magic School Bus: In the Time of the Dinosaurs.** Scholastic, 1994.

Henderson, Douglas. **Dinosaur Tree.** Bradbury Press, 1994.

Lindsay, William. **Prehistoric Life.** Knopf, 1994.

Taylor, Paul. **Fossil.** Knopf, 1990.

The Visual Dictionary of Prehistoric Life. Dorling Kindersley, 1995.

Organizations and Online Sites

The American Museum of Natural History
Central Park West at
79th Street
New York, NY 10024
http://www.amnh.org

One of the world's largest natural-history museums, with exceptional collections on dinosaurs and fossils. Its website has a special *Stegosaurus* page.

Dinorama
*http://www.
nationalgeographic.com/
dinorama/frame.html/*

A National Geographic site with information about dinosaurs and current methods of learning about them. Includes timelines, animations, and fun facts.

Dinosaur National Monument
4545 Highway 40
Dinosaur, CO 81610-9724
http://www.nps.gov/dino/

Visit a unique natural exhibit of more than 1,600 dinosaur bones deposited in an ancient riverbed turned to stone.

National Museum of Natural History, Smithsonian Institution
10th Street and
Constitution Ave. NW
*Washington, D.C.
http://www.mnh.si.edu/
nmnhweb.html*

In the museum's Dinosaur Hall, you can see—and in one case touch—real fossils of dinosaurs.

ZoomDinosaurs
*http://www.
ZoomDinosaurs.com/*

A site that contains everything you might want to know about dinosaurs and other ancient reptiles. Its *Stegosaurus* page includes facts, myths, activities, a geologic time chart, printouts, and links.

Important Words

asteroid rocky, planetlike object orbiting in space

blood vessel tube in the body through which blood flows

catastrophic involving a great and sudden violent change or disaster

comet frozen ball of water, gases, and dust from the farthest reaches of our solar system

digested changed into a form usable by the body

extinct no longer in existence

predator animal that preys on another animal for food

reconstructed put back together again

remains bones or tissue left behind after an animal or plant dies

staggered placed in a zigzag arrangement

Index

Meet the Author

Elaine Landau has a Bachelor of Arts degree in English and Journalism from New York University and a Master's degree in Library and Information Science from Pratt Institute. She has worked as a newspaper reporter, a children's book editor, and a youth services librarian, but especially enjoys writing for young people.

Ms. Landau has written more than a hundred nonfiction books on various topics. She lives in Miami, Florida, with her husband, Norman, and son, Michael.